# Who You Gonna Call?

# Responding to a Medical Emergency with the Strategic National Stockpile

Stephen D. Prior, Ph.D.

Director, National Security Health Policy Center

Potomac Institute for Policy Studies

**Report Commissioned by the**

**National Defense University**

**Center for Technology and National Security Policy**

**June 2004**

The views expressed in this article are those of the authors and do not reflect the official policy or position of the National Defense University, the Department of Defense, or the U.S. Government. All information and sources for this paper were drawn from unclassified materials.

**Stephen D. Prior** is the Director, National Security Health Policy Center at the Potomac Institute for Policy Studies. Dr. Prior may be contacted via e-mail at sprior@potomacinstitute.org or by phone at (703) 525-0770.

# Executive Summary

Prior to the terrorist attacks of September 11, 2001 and the subsequent anthrax attacks, the Strategic National Stockpile (SNS), known as the National Pharmaceutical Stockpile until March 2003, was an important component of the national medical response to a crisis, but one that had not yet been tested in a real emergency. That changed in the fall of 2001. Since the terrorist attacks against the World Trade Center buildings and the Pentagon, and the later anthrax episodes, the cost of the SNS has grown from a roughly $50 million asset to one worth more than $600 million.

The SNS is designed to supplement state and local public health agencies in the event of a biological or chemical terrorism incident anywhere and at anytime in the United States or its territories. Federal authorities do not consider the stockpile a first-response tool. Rather, its purpose is to bolster the response of a state or city government to a biological or chemical attack or other medical emergency that requires additional resources.

The SNS is managed jointly by the Departments of Homeland Security (DHS) and Health and Human Services (HHS). Its use is coordinated through the Centers for Disease Control and Prevention (CDC), one of the major operating components of HHS. The stockpile comprises 12 separate "push packages," each capable of reaching its designated destination within 12 hours of DHS authorization. Each push package includes caches of pharmaceuticals, antidotes, and medical supplies designed to provide a broad spectrum of assets in the early hours of an event. The push packages are positioned in strategically located, secure warehouses and delivered by commercial, express carriers. Additional, specially tailored supplies known as vendor managed inventory (VMI) can follow within 24 to 36 hours of an event.

This paper reviews the history and current status of the SNS, provides an overview of its role in incident response, and reports on the testing of SNS deployment in recent terrorism exercises. The paper also explores some of the regulatory and legal issues that surround the use of the SNS and examines the dependence of the U.S. military on SNS supplies during crisis and consequence management support to civilians in the United States.

# Table of Contents

# History

The vulnerability of human populations to diseases has been extensively documented by many authors and does not need to be addressed in this article. Following the emergence of HIV/AIDS and, more recently, the dual threats of a man-made incident, exemplified by the anthrax attacks of fall 2001, and the threat from a naturally occurring disease, exemplified by the 2003 SARS and West Nile virus outbreaks, response to a medical crisis has become a topic of significant concern. Particular attention was paid to the reliance of local and state health responders on support from Federal agencies. The response of the Federal agencies to emerging threats has likewise become an issue for discussion and has prompted new and innovative solutions to a massive influx of funds over the past five years. In 1999, the United States Congress tasked the Department of Health and Human Services (HHS) and its Centers for Disease Control and Prevention (CDC) with establishing a National Pharmaceutical Stockpile (NPS) that could resupply large quantities of essential medical materiel to states and communities during an emergency within 12 hours of a Federal decision to deploy.[1] The specific mission described under the congressional mandate required that the CDC address the NPS to:

"An act of terrorism (or a large scale natural disaster) targeting the U.S. civilian population [that] will require rapid access to large quantities of pharmaceuticals and medical supplies." The CDC responded by developing both a stockpile of materiel and a means of rapid deployment that could meet the stated requirements. Within two years, the response capability was tested.

## *First Deployment*

Immediately after the September 11, 2001 terrorist attacks, the CDC dispatched a 50-ton, preassembled push package of supplies, pharmaceuticals, and medical equipment to New York City. "Each package," according to HHS, "involved several truckloads of materials and was intended to be sufficient to respond to an emergency involving mass casualties." The push package arrived within 7 hours of HHS Secretary Tommy

---

[1] See CDC website: http://www.bt.cdc.gov/stockpile/. Accessed February 2004.

Thompson's order to deploy. Three of the four airplanes in American airspace the night of September 11 supported the SNS program; the fourth was Air Force One.

Figure 1 – A single "push package" weighs 94,424 pounds and fills either one wide-body aircraft or seven tractor trailers. The Strategic National Stockpile program pledges to deliver the pre-packaged supplies within 12 hours of the Federal (DHS) decision to deploy. *Source: Centers for Disease Control and Prevention, Atlanta, GA.*

### Second Deployment

On October 8, 2001, the CDC again tapped the stockpile to ship 100 cases of anti-infectives by air to Florida's Palm Beach County Health Department in Boca Raton. Exposure to *Bacillus anthracis*, the bacterium that causes anthrax, had been confirmed in two men. On the recommendations of state and local public health officials and an onsite team of CDC investigators, the CDC supplied Palm Beach County enough anti-infectives, primarily doxycycline and fluoroquinolones, to treat thousands of people, if necessary. The CDC deployed the anti-infectives to Florida without enlisting one of the assembled push packages. The Palm Beach County scare showcased the utility of the stockpile's vendor managed inventory; by October 10, more than 700 people had been evaluated at a local health clinic, and antibiotics had been distributed.

## Expansion Since 2001

Since these initial uses, the stockpile has grown to become a repository of anti-infectives, chemical antidotes, antitoxins, life-support medications, IV administration and airway maintenance supplies, surgical items, and other medical supplies.[2]

The DHS defines the function of the SNS as providing a means "To ensure availability and rapid deployment of life-saving pharmaceuticals, antidotes, other medical supplies, and equipment necessary to counter the effects of nerve agents, biological pathogens, and chemical agents."

Funding for the SNS reflects the critical role it has in the planning of responses to any future incident. In fiscal years 1999-2002, funding for the stockpile hovered just above $50 million; following the attacks of fall 2001, the funding grew more than ten-fold—the stockpile was now truly a national resource.[3]

## Role of the SNS

The stockpile is designed to *supplement* state and local public health agencies in the event of a biological or chemical terrorism incident anywhere and at anytime in the United States or its territories; it is *not* a first-response tool. Rather, its purpose is to bolster the response of a state or city government to a biological or chemical attack or other medical emergency where additional resources are required.[4] This augmentation approach has obvious implications for the choice of products included in the push packages and the vendor managed inventory. The stockpile focuses on providing resources relevant to an incident that has progressed beyond the initial medical resources of a locality or state. Clearly, this is not ideal for all incidents, especially those that require very rapid responses, such as release of a chemical agent. This has led to some revisions of the content and deployment of the stockpile. One future initiative is the proposed Chempack Program, the HHS plan to supply local fire departments and emergency medical services with antidotes for organophosphates and cyanide prior to

---

[2] Some of these components, for example medical countermeasures against chemical warfare agents, were included in the stockpile prior to September 2001.
[3] FY'99-$51M, FY'00-$52M, FY'01-$52M, FY'02-$645M, FY'03-$300M.
[4] SNS supplies also are available in the event of naturally occurring incidents, such as hurricanes, floods, and natural disease outbreaks.

deployment, rather than as part of a push package. This means that the antidotes can be sent aboard responding ambulances and fire trucks to be used within the short time frame after exposure to hazardous material.[5]

With the creation of the Department of Homeland Security, the role of the NPS and its management was revisited. The Homeland Security Act of 2002 charged the DHS with defining the program's goals and gave the department responsibility for stockpile funding and deployment. In March 2003, the NPS became the Strategic National Stockpile under joint management of the DHS and HHS. (The evolution of the SNS and VMI is depicted in Figure 2.)

With the Nation's threat level constantly elevated, the SNS has become critically important. As new drugs are developed, HHS evaluates whether they are vital to national security and, together with the DHS determines whether they should be added to the stockpile.

### Vendor Managed Inventory

The SNS has been supplemented by a second tier of medical products that are under the control and management of selected, pre-qualified vendors. The so-called vendor managed inventory (VMI) is designed to arrive 24-36 hours after SNS deployment, and to provide for specific medical requirements such as targeted antibiotics. VMI offers significant value if the threat is well-defined, because the pharmaceuticals and supplies can be tailored specific to the suspected or confirmed agent or agents. In this instance, the DHS may decide to ship only VMI and not a push package, as was the case for the October 2001 Palm Beach County shipment. VMI supplies are considered a component of the SNS and do not require separate request or consent dialogues. Pharmaceuticals in both the push packages and VMI are rotated so that the inventories never reach their expiration dates and always remain within their extended shelf life.

---

[5] "Many of us felt that there was no point in having kits in the stockpile when they need to be used in the first minutes and hours after exposure and the stockpile is not designed to get to a city for six to twelve hours, [so] we gave those out to communities all over the country," said Dr. Jerry Hauer, former director of the HHS Office of Emergency Preparedness, in the September 2003 issue of *U.S. Medicine* Newspaper ("HHS Office Directs Agency's Anti-Bioterrorism Efforts" by Stephen Spotswood).

# Strategic National Stockpile - Timeline

| | 1998 | 1999 | 2000 | 2001 | 2002 | 2003 | 2004 |
|---|---|---|---|---|---|---|---|
| **Instances of Use** | | | | • 11 September: Push Package dispatched to site of NYC tragedy<br>• 8 October: Anti-infectives shipped to Boca Raton, FL | | | |
| **Legislation** | • May: Presidential Decision Directive 62, VA & USPHS to ensure stockpiles of antidotes maintained nationwide | • Congress tasks HHS with Bioterrorism Preparedness & Response Program (BPRP), including creation of NPS | | | • 7 August: Fiscal 2002 Supplemental Appropriations Act includes $593 Mil for aquisition of NPS supplies<br>• 25 November: President signs "Homeland Security Act," creating new dept (DHS) & transferring Stockpile mgt | | |
| **Status** | | • 29 October: GAO Report, "Chemical & Biological Medical Supplies Are Poorly Managed"<br>• December: First Push Package Assembled | • CDC raises mandate from four Push Packages to eight | • NPS nation's premiere owner of smallpox vaccine<br>• 1 May: GAO Report, "Accountability Over Medical Supplies Needs Further Improvement"<br>• CDC raises mandate from eight Push Packages to twelve | • Anthrax treatment capacity raised from 2 million to 12 millions persons<br>• Potassium iodide made available to S/L agencies for storage in public facilities<br>• DOD "Shelf-life Extension Program" developed through FDA<br>• "Chempack Project" outlined: forward placement of nerve agent antidotes for S/L response | • 28 January: President introduces proposed "BioShield" program during annual "State of the Union" address<br>• 1 March: DHS assumes joint management of Stockpile; NPS renamed SNS | • 18 February: USPS announces developing doorstep delivery plan<br>• Chempacks to be delivered to 59 BT project areas |
| **Exercises** | | | • May: TOPOFF 1 largest counter-terrorism exercise ever held in US | • June: "Dark Winter" tabletop exercise | | • 12 May - 16 May: TOPOFF 2 assesses reactions of responders and leaders during simulated release of WMD in 2 US cities<br>• November: "Scarlet Cloud" tabletop exercise | |
| **Budget** | FY 99 - $51 Mil. | FY 00 - $52 Mil. | FY 01 - $52 Mil. | FY 02 - $645 Mil.* | FY 03 - $300 Mil. | FY 04 - $400 Mil. | |

**Figure 2 – The stockpile's history includes a substantial upgrade in funding following the events of September 11, 2001.**

# Current Status

The responsibility of the DHS/CDC is to deliver either push package or VMI assets to an affected site for use after local supplies have been depleted. The onus is on local and state authorities to repackage stocks for individual dosing and to distribute doses at sites within the "hot zone." To that end, it is critical that local authorities draft SNS deployment plans before a bioterrorist attack, so that lack of local organization does not hamper the rapid distribution of pharmaceuticals. The logistical burden on the local and state responders who receive, dispense, and distribute the SNS is considerable. The time and manpower costs for this activity are significant and include requirements for security and personnel accreditation that will stretch the capacity and capabilities of most local and state authorities. Recent experiences with exercises that involve the SNS (or the notional use of the SNS) have demonstrated the difficulties that are inherent in distributing the SNS materiel over the "last mile" to the target population.

The SNS currently consists of 12 push packages, each identical in content and capable of providing support to a variety of threats. These caches of pharmaceuticals, antidotes, and medical supplies are designed to provide rapid delivery of a broad spectrum of assets in the early hours of an event. They consist of:

- **Antibiotics:** doxycycline, ciprofloxacin, gentamicin, erythromycin

- **Other medications:** dopamine, epinephrine, albuterol inhaler, morphine, lorazepam

- **Medical/surgical supplies:** sterile water for injection, NaCl flush, syringes/needles/catheters, IV solutions, tape/dressings/gauze/tourniquet

- **Airway management supplies:** oxygen masks/tubing, manual resuscitators (bag-valve-mask), ventilators and suction units

- **Other:** tablet counting machines, power strips, extension cords, duct tape, plastic zip bags, data collection sheets

The push packages are positioned in environmentally controlled, secured warehouses in secret locations strategically sited around the Nation and ready for immediate delivery by UPS and FedEx to any affected area. The goal is to have the resources onsite within 12 hours of the Federal decision to deploy.

Push packages occupy 124 cargo containers, weigh 94,424 pounds, and require 5,000 square feet of floor space for proper staging and management. A package fills a wide-body aircraft or seven tractor trailers. Follow-on, vendor managed inventory (VMI) supplies can arrive 24 to 36 hours after the event. The SNS is described in great detail—including extensive information on receipt, distribution, and dispensing—in a CDC *Guide for Planners.*[6]

Purchases of pharmaceuticals and medical supplies for the Federal stockpile are made by the Department of Veterans Affairs (VA), according to the General Accounting Office (GAO), which has been issuing reports on the stockpile since 1999. The VA also manages the contracts for storage, rotation, security, and transportation of stocks. Quarterly quality insurance/quality control checks, annual 100 percent inventory, and inspection of environmental conditions, security, and package maintenance are performed to keep packages, including VMI, in top condition.

---

[6] *Receiving, Distributing, and Dispensing the National Pharmaceutical Stockpile: A Guide for Planners – Version 9* (Atlanta, GA: Centers for Disease Control, April 2002).

# Role of the SNS in Incident Response

### Requesting the Strategic National Stockpile

Figure 3 illustrates the process for requesting SNS supplies. The decision to deploy is a collaborative effort between local, state, and Federal officials. Local officials who identify a potential or actual problem that will exceed the resource capacity should contact their health department or state emergency management officials, who in turn can alert the governor, who can request the SNS directly through the DHS/CDC or as part of a formal request for Federal assistance through the national emergency response system.

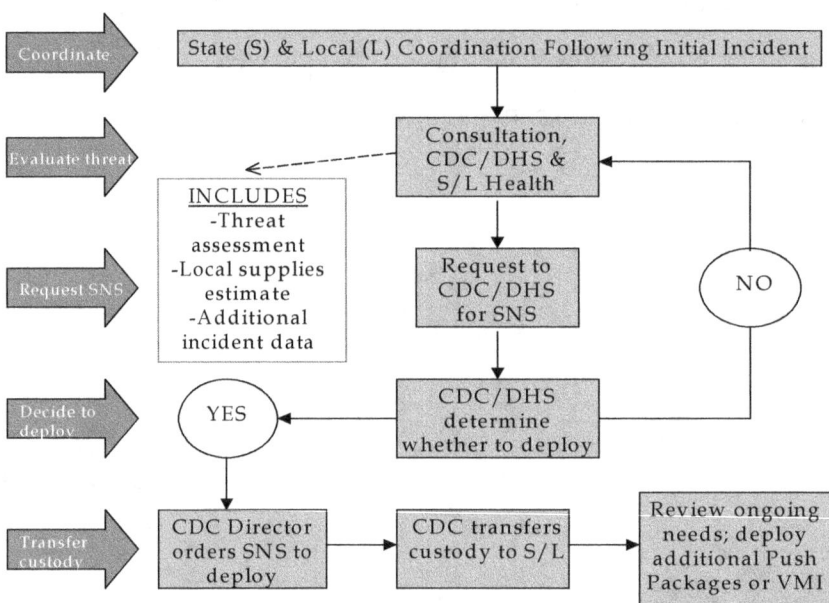

**Figure 3 – The tiered decision-making and communication process allows for express delivery of medical supplies and prevents a hasty or unwarranted call to arms.**

The director of the CDC will quickly evaluate the request; if local resources are deemed insufficient, the SNS will be deployed. Not all requests will result in SNS deployment. While the CDC has the lead role in deployment of the SNS, the DHS, because of its functional expertise, is the nominal and legal lead. The CDC will assume the lead in deploying the SNS for local use, but coordination with the DHS remains an essential element of an effective response.

The requirement for collaboration at the local, state, and Federal level means that effective deployment of the SNS will need an expedited communication process between all parties. This is an area where exercises and testing of the plans, policies, and procedures on an ongoing basis can be of great value—any local or state exercise involving an incident that could require the deployment of the SNS would benefit from specific assessment of how the request would be coordinated by the various parties.

### Storage and Deployment

Push packages are described as containing "a little bit of everything" to augment local supplies and meet general emergency needs. If a locality knows in advance the specific pharmaceuticals it needs, it may request aid from the VMI component of the SNS. VMI is a cushion that can be accessed rapidly in times of crisis. Emergency supplies of ciprofloxacin, for example, were made available from VMI in the wake of the 2001 anthrax exposures. After the delivery of a push package, follow-on supplies from VMI are delivered within 24-36 hours of the initial request. Alternatively, VMI may serve as an initial, tailored response to an event involving a known agent. VMI also provides a means by which the government can limit the cost of buying, storing, and managing stocks. Costs would increase if the government purchased materials that it ultimately had to destroy because they were too much to reinsert into ordinary medical distribution channels.

The CDC website indicates that state and local authorities repackage bulk medicines and label them and other medical supplies in accordance with the state's terrorism contingency plans. The CDC transfers authority for the materials to state and local authorities on arrival. It also provides a Technical Advisory Response Unit (TARU), a team of 5 or 6 pharmacists, emergency responders, and logistics experts, to assist state and local officials when stockpiled supplies are deployed.[7]

---

[7] Twelve TARU teams exist, each assigned to a different push package, and all based at the CDC's headquarters in Atlanta, Georgia.

The delivery and receipt of a push package is a complex, collaborative effort that requires significant coordination. The best time to plan and train for such an effort is now, rather than during the next crisis. The need for proactive planning cannot be over-emphasized; lack of planning remains a potential point of weakness for many locations around the nation. The state and local responsibilities for the SNS can vary from state to state. Not all states have resolved how to deal with the SNS. One area of concern is the fact that some states with extensive military air bases incorrectly believe that using these facilities offers the best route for SNS receipt and local distribution. The CDC advises that "military airfields (are) the absolutely last alternative," for reasons discussed below.

By whatever means, delivery of packages is a significant logistical challenge. The CDC guidance is that the initial site for receipt, storage, and staging of the SNS requires 12,000 square feet of floor space and must include temperature/humidity control, emergency electrical power, security, and an area for storage of controlled substances. Push packages contain three controlled substances: morphine, diazepam, and lorazepam. While they only occupy approximately 18 cubic feet of the package, they require considerable control and regulation in terms of distribution. Any person handling or using the drugs, even under conditions of crisis, must be registered with the Drug Enforcement Agency.

### Distribution

Distribution of stocks is the responsibility of the state or locality that receives the push packages. It is often recommended that after receipt of the package the state use its agencies—state police, National Guard, etc.—to coordinate the staging, distribution, and dispensing of SNS materials. For instance, it would seem sensible to task law enforcement agencies to provide security for the push package. This type of coordination needs to be planned ahead of time, and the tasks that require support should be made clear to all parties. Equally, the use of state and local resources will help in ensuring that there is adequate and effective communication between the various parties engaged in distribution of the push package contents.

When the CDC deployed the National Pharmaceutical Stockpile after the terrorist attacks in the fall of 2001, most of the medications were in bulk containers of thousands of tablets and capsules, which poses a problem when trying to dispense prescription drugs in an emergency situation. Since then the stockpile has been modified. The CDC contracted vendors to package 50 percent of the anti-infective stocks, including doxycycline, ciprofloxacin, and amoxicillin, into 10- or 25-day-supply, unit-of-use bottles that are replicas of the larger manufacturer-made containers. Each push package now contains two high-speed, industrial repackaging machines that can produce 5,000 unit-of-use sealed bags of medications per hour. Although a TARU will assist workers and operate machines if necessary, the mission's efficiency depends heavily on local infrastructure and planning. The TARU team cannot expediently distribute the mass of supplies and equipment without highly trained emergency management workers on hand to greet them. The CDC also has updated its stockpile guide with new information that includes dispensing information for the medications.[8]

### *Utilization*

Because of the need to cover many eventualities, the SNS will provide more of some materials than are required for response to an incident. This leaves an issue of leftover supplies. Under normal circumstances, the CDC expects leftover stockpile supplies to be absorbed by the local health care system and used by community and state medical personnel, rather than shipped back to their point of origin. It is possible however, that unused supplies could be returned to the CDC, if materials had been stored properly and had not been compromised. Reabsorbtion of SNS materials would be assessed on a case-by-case basis. The materials that are supplied in the SNS are meticulously packaged and configured in a certain manner. If that configuration is compromised in any way or if any of the boxes are unsealed, those materials are not returned to the stockpile.

With respect to VMI, it is also possible for the CDC to resell to the vendors unused medical supplies and pharmaceuticals, as long as they are at least six months from their expiration date and still in the sealed, original packages.

---

[8] The CDC guide is not available to the general public, but pharmacists may obtain a copy by requesting it from a local emergency management or public health agency.

# Role of State and Local Responders

The national exercises that have incorporated assessment for the deployment of the SNS included TOPOFF 2. In May 2003, the Department of Homeland Security and the Department of State, in cooperation with Federal, state, local, and Canadian partners, completed a five-day, full-scale exercise and simulation of how the Nation would respond in the event of a weapons of mass destruction (WMD) attack. The exercise consisted of simulated attacks in the Chicago and Seattle metropolitan areas. There remain somewhat conflicting reports about the efficiency with which the SNS was deployed and distributed during exercise play. In general, it appears that the activation, deployment, and distribution of the SNS were extensively played during TOPOFF 2.

The exercise tested the ability of all levels of government to make decisions, allocate resources, coordinate and communicate, and inform the public regarding this critical SNS resource. The state of Illinois tested its ability to break down and secure the antibiotic stocks. Local jurisdictions tested their abilities to distribute supplies of antibiotics to their first responders and citizens. Overall, the request, receipt, breakdown, distribution, and dispensing of the SNS during the exercise were completed successfully. It is important to note, however, that the exercise includes significant artificialities that make the simplify and detach the process from the problems that may occur during deployment in a real crisis.[9] Findings from TOPOFF 2 include the following: Determining a prophylaxis distribution policy for first responders and citizenry across local jurisdictions was challenging. This was due, in part, to the enormous logistical challenges of distributing medications to a large metropolitan area, as well as the very real limitation of the amount of medication that was immediately available. Inconsistent information was given by different jurisdictions as to the locations of the suspected plague release sites, as well as who should seek prophylaxis and when.

The bifurcated roles and responsibilities of HHS (CDC) and the DHS were another area of concern.[10] During TOPOFF 2, officials at HHS and the DHS were uncertain about how to meet a state request for disaster medical supplies. As a result, regional and national officials were unable to respond rapidly to an urgent request for

---

[9] Similar concerns have been expressed in other exercises that involve SNS "play" – it is very difficult to recreate the reality of a crisis during large scale exercises that have been months in the planning.
[10] See http://healthlinks.washington.edu/nwcphp/nph/f2003/may_f2003.pdf. Accessed March 2004.

supplies from the Strategic National Stockpile. Federal government officials insisted that the request for supplies come from the governor, despite the governor having already announced a Declaration of Emergency and a formal request for assistance under the Stafford Act.[11] It was recommended that the DHS and HHS sort out these responsibilities and provide clear instructions to state health officials on how to obtain supplemental medical supplies in times of emergency.[12] The publication of the Interim National Response Plan (Interim NRP) in September 2003 clarified these issues.[13] The Interim NRP supercedes the Federal Response Plan and other Federal emergency response plans. Under the Interim NRP, HHS remains responsible for execution of Emergency Support Function Eight.[14] This issue has sometimes been a source of confusion because while the Office of Emergency Response—the HHS organization responsible for managing ESF-8 responsibilities—was transferred to the DHS, the responsibility for execution of ESF-8 was assigned to HHS as a department, and is still retained by HHS under the Interim NRP. While there remains ambiguity regarding the exact lines of that authority, the Secretary of HHS believes that he retains considerable legal authority for decisions to deploy the SNS.[15] Some of the current ambiguity is scheduled to disappear next fiscal year, since the Administration's budget returns funding and ownership of the SNS to HHS starting in FY'05.[16]

In recent months further exercises have been held that focus on the deployment and distribution of the SNS. According to published reports, "Scarlet Cloud" an exercise hosted by the National Defense University (NDU) in November 2003, showed that the government still "needed to improve plans for delivering vaccines and antibiotics."[17] It is clear that the continued emphasis on this aspect of a response to an escalating incident will result in improved plans, policies, and procedures for effectively using the SNS.

## Regulatory and Legal Issues with the SNS

---

[11] The Robert T. Stafford Disaster Relief and Emergency Assistance Act. U.S. Public Law 93-288 and amendments, known as "The Stafford Act."

[12] Excerpt from "TOPOFF Exercise Offers Lessons for Preparedness" by Susan May (http://healthlinks.washington.edu/nwcphp/nph/f2003/may_f2003.pdf).

[13] Interim National Response Plan. See http://www.uscg.mil/hq/g-o/g-opr/NRP%20Initial%20signed%2022Oct03.pdf. Accessed February 2004.

[14] Emergency Support Function Eight provides coordinated Federal assistance to supplement state and local resources in response to public health and medical care needs following a major disaster or emergency, or during a developing medical situation.

[15] Personal communication with Dr. Seth Carus, Center for Counterproliferation Research, National Defense University.

[16] Ibid.

[17] "U.S. Has New Concerns About Anthrax Readiness," Judith Miller, December 28, 2003, *The New York Times*.

Several issues related to legal and regulatory requirements impact the SNS, including liability and labeling practices, distribution of controlled substances, and the likelihood that the United States military will become engaged during the medical emergency.

### *Liability and Indemnification*

Almost without exception, the use of any medical product can produce unintended side effects that may cause injury or harm to the patient. By extension, the SNS has the potential not only to do great good but also to cause unintended harm. This is even more likely to be the case if the SNS is deployed on the basis of its use in prophylaxis of persons who may or may not have been exposed to a harmful agent. In the anthrax attacks of 2001, the use of antibiotics for prophylaxis was extended to over 35,000 people through the use of VMI. The vast majority of these people had probably not been exposed to anthrax, but because exposure could not be ruled out in most cases, the decision was made to provide antibiotics. As noted above, the use of antibiotics by otherwise healthy persons led to discussion of the side effects, which in turn led to examination of the legal liability issues that may result from any harm done to the antibiotic recipients.[18] One of the key issues under discussion was the question of whether or not, in deploying the SNS and advising on its use, the Federal government or its agents were exposed to legal liability and the attendant possibility of being sued for damages by persons who had experienced side effects from the use of antibiotics.

In a comprehensive review of vaccine liability, J.S. Mair and M. Mair explored legal issues that may impact use of antibiotics or other medical materiel from the SNS.[19] They noted, "under the historic legal doctrine that 'the king can do no wrong,' the Federal government is immune from all liability and cannot be sued without its consent. Recognizing the inherent inequities that resulted from such sweeping protection, the Federal government has waived its sovereign immunity in some circumstances. With the enactment of the Federal Tort Claims Act (FTCA) in 1946, the Federal government agreed to substitute itself as defendant when Federal employees, who were acting within

---

[18] This issue is addressed in "Antimicrobial Post-exposure Prophylaxis for Anthrax: Adverse Events and Adherence," C.W. Shepard et al. *Emerging Infectious Diseases*, Vol. 8 No. 10, October 2002.

[19] "Vaccine Liability in the Era of Bioterrorism," JS Mair & M Mair. *Biosecurity & Bioterrorism* 1(3): 169-184, 2003.

the scope of their office or employment, are sued in tort. Tort has been defined as a 'private or civil wrong or injury, including action for bad faith breach of contract, for which the court will provide a remedy in the form of an action for damages.' When the government substitutes itself as defendant under the FTCA, Federal employees cannot be sued in tort and special rules govern the lawsuit."

Mair and Mair identified several precedents that relate to handling vaccine liability that may also be applied to other SNS materiel. They noted that these are not always mutually exclusive. The government can 1) substitute itself as defendant and accept liability on behalf of the participants in the vaccination program, 2) decide that no one needs to be held liable and establish a no-fault compensation program, 3) indemnify (i.e., reimburse) vaccine manufacturers and distributors, providers, and other participants after they have been sued and a judgment issued against them, or 4) alter the normal rules of litigation and/or compensation.

Of particular note, given the current legal status of the SNS within the DHS, is the language in the Homeland Security Act that speaks to liability following administration of medical products. Government liability is expressly addressed by Section 304 of the Act, which applies only to "covered countermeasures against smallpox." If the same vaccines and treatments are used for a pathogen other than smallpox—for example, monkeypox—Section 304 does not apply. Moreover, if vaccines or treatments are developed or used for other possible bioterrorism agents (e.g., bacteria such as plague, toxins such as botulinum, viruses such as ebola, etc.), the Act must be amended or a new law enacted.

### *Labeling*

State and Federal regulations specify the information that must be provided on a drug label and the information sheet that will be provided to patients or the public if drugs are to be used as prophylactics. For example, the Food and Drug Administration (FDA) requires that the label include drug name, strength, and quantity, directions for use, location of dispensing facility, serial number of the prescription, date, and the name of the prescriber. The information on the labels of the products in the SNS can vary greatly. Most are limited to the drug name, strength, quantity, lot number, and unique prescription number. The local sites must provide the additional data that is required to conform to Federal and state law.[20]

When bulk drugs in the SNS are repackaged on-site, the labeling machines that accompany each of the push packs can be programmed to provide the required labeling. However, even under these circumstances, the dispensing site will have to annotate the patient's name on the label. According to the planner's guide, maximum repackaging of a push package requires 300 volunteers for 8-10 hours.[21] This would produce 27,800 individual regimens per hour and provide the capacity needed to dispense the SNS bulk products to the public in appropriate unit doses. Clearly, handling the SNS is a formidable logistic challenge.

### Distribution of Controlled Substances

The three controlled substances in push packs (morphine, diazepam, and lorazepam) not only require special, secure storage conditions, but also legal considerations during delivery, storage, and dispensing. The Drug Enforcement Administration (DEA) provides a system of registration for all persons who must handle specific classes of controlled substances, and this applies to the SNS. A detailed chain-of-custody must be kept, and transfer of materials from registrant to registrant must be carefully documented. It also is suggested that these materials be transferred in coordination with law enforcement agencies to provide security for the products and the dispensing personnel.

### IND and Off-Label Use of Strategic National Stockpile Materiel

According to the CDC, all drugs in the SNS have long-established safety and efficacy records. However, some are not FDA-labeled (that is, licensed) to treat specific agents that may be released in a biological incident.[22] The CDC is working with the FDA to establish a process that will qualify these drugs, but until the specific labeling is approved, they may have to be used under the auspices of an Investigational New Drug

---

[20] Current 12-hour push packs contain the following prepackaged, labeled, individual 10-day regimens of oral antibiotics: 85,000 bottles ciprofloxacin (20 tablets); 85,000 bottles doxycycline (20 tablets); and 25,000 bottles amoxicillin (60 tablets).
[21] Repackaging a 12-hour push pack current bulk tablets will protect 148,00 people with a 10-day regimen or 496,000 people with a 3-day regimen.

(IND) application. The use of SNS materiel under an IND presents some interesting and potentially problematic logistical and legal issues.

One issue is whether the U.S. government can legally stockpile medical countermeasures for purposes that are not identified on the label of the product. This was a significant point of contention between the CDC and the FDA before and after the 9/11 attacks . The standard treatment for some diseases in ordinary medical practice is off-label (i.e., the drug is being used to treat a disease for which it is not specifically licensed by the FDA). For example, for plague the drug of choice is a generic antibiotic. The FDA license for such drugs does not contain specific reference to its use in treatment of plague; thus, use in treatment of plague is off-label. The FDA contended that the CDC could not stockpile products for such off-label uses.

These concerns led to the invention of the "Emergency Use Authorization" contained in the Bioshield legislation first proposed by the Administration in February 2003. That authorization would allow for an emergency declaration that would permit waivers to the usual procedures for dispensing drugs under IND regulations. The requirement to use an IND for administration of certain drugs for specific diseases would also mean that each person who is receiving the drug would need to read and sign a consent form that meets FDA IND requirements. This requirement will need to be fulfilled at the time and place of the dispensing of the drug and will impose a significant logistical burden on local responders, who already will be facing a significant task in dispensing the SNS materiel to a (potentially) large affected population. The logistical burden associated with the use of SNS drugs under an IND will include the need to use a patient-tracking capability to gather data on any adverse reactions to the drugs.

An example of an innovative solution to off-label use is cited by the CDC in the guide for receiving, distributing, and dispensing the NPS.[23] It relates to the issue of expiration dates for SNS drugs. Before the fall 2001 attacks, bulk drugs could not be repackaged and retain their original manufacturer's expiration date. This meant that repackaged bulk drugs had a much shorter lifespan. After the attacks, the CDC "located firms that operated under a special FDA license and were able to create unit-of-use regimens that keep their original manufacturer's expiration date."

---

[22] Examples of IND use of SNS products cited by the CDC include the use of ciprofloxacin for tularemia and amoxicillin for anthrax.

Recently, the FDA has coordinated with the CDC to ensure that gentamicin (an antimicrobial drug) has a swifter IND process.[24] In an effort to have SNS stocks adequately labeled, the FDA and CDC have worked to identify those requiring an IND application and have created the concept of the "streamlined" IND, which meets regulatory requirements and allows access to SNS resources in the event of a terrorist attack. Other drugs identified and relabeled by the FDA for emergency non-IND use include ciprofloxacin, another antibiotic long used for inhalation anthrax.[25] Shortly after the anthrax attacks, the Center for Drug Evaluation and Research (CDER) worked to relabel doxycycline and procaine penicillin for post-exposure management of anthrax.

### Military Use of the Strategic National Stockpile

The Department of Defense (DOD) has no formal role in the storage, deployment, or utilization of the SNS. However, it is likely that, in the event of SNS deployment, some elements of the DOD will become engaged. As noted above, although military bases seem to provide secure landing sites and facilities for the initial delivery of the SNS, they should be used only as a last resort.[26] There are two principal reasons for this. First, during a crisis that requires SNS deployment, most nearby military facilities will be operating under heightened levels of security and will not be freely accessible to civilians. Second, most military airfields are unable to offload a wide-bodied commercial jetliner, and the use of alternative means of offload would delay deployment of stocks.

If the military does not receive the SNS, the first DOD engagement with the SNS is likely to be when National Guard units, under the control of the governor, play their part in a local or state response plan. The use of Guard units in state and local responses to an emerging incident is an essential part of most state plans for crisis and consequence management. This is true whether the incident is man-made or naturally occurring. The role of the Guard with respect to the SNS will vary from state to state but might include support to civil authorities in law enforcement, security, logistics, or the use of DOD-specific skills or resources.

---

[23] *Receiving, Distributing, and Dispensing the National Pharmaceutical Stockpile: A Guide for Planners – Version 9* (Atlanta GA: CDC, April 2002).

[24] See http://www.usmedicine.com/article.cfm?articleID=731&issueID=54. Accessed February 2004.

[25] Ciprofloxacin had already been labeled for anthrax treatment by the time the toxic substance began arriving in the mail in October 2001.

Regardless of the role that the Guard plays, it is likely that the Guard units will include personnel requiring access to the SNS. For example, if antibiotic prophylaxis is being used in the civilian population, the Guard probably will share SNS stocks with civilians. However, it is worth noting that unlike their civilian counterparts, Guard personnel will likely have been vaccinated against some of the possible biological agents, such as smallpox and anthrax. They also will be well versed in the use of individual protective equipment (IPE), such as masks, respirators, and suits; collective protective equipment (ColPro), such as shelters and over-pressure vehicles; and military detection equipment, such as the Chemical Agent Monitor (CAM). Clearly, the role of the Guard in incidents involving weapons of mass destruction (WMD) will be critically important.

The deployment of DOD assets other than the National Guard for homeland defense operations is the responsibility of U.S. Northern Command (USNORTHCOM).[27] These DOD components probably would be deployed according to the DOD directive on military assistance to civil authorities (MACA).[28] This would occur when a state requests support from Federal authorities under the auspices of legislative authority, such as the Stafford Act, which operates in the event of a Federal emergency or some other form of declared disaster. MACA can provide a wide range of resources and assets, from unskilled manpower to skilled and qualified personnel and specialized equipment. In this case, the DOD anticipates that operating MACA will grant military access to the SNS materiel. The alternative would be that the DOD might consider establishing its own, scaled-down version of the SNS with materiel that is tailored to the specific requirements of a DOD deployment. Current DOD assets include:

- DOD anthrax vaccine stockpile at BioPort, Lansing, Michigan

- DOD smallpox vaccine stockpile at CDC SNS locations (classified locations)

- DOD botulinum antitoxin stockpiles, Fort Detrick, Maryland and Europe

Selected military-specific supplies, such as MARK 1 kits and field dressings items, are kept in a few Defense Logistics Agency warehouses around the country. Also,

---

[26] *Receiving, Distributing, and Dispensing the National Pharmaceutical Stockpile: A Guide for Planners – Version 9* (Atlanta GA: CDC, April 2002).

[27] See http//www northcom.mil/index.cfm?fuseaction=s.who_civil. Accessed February 2004.

[28] DOD Directive 3025.15, "Military Assistance to Civil Authorities", February 18, 1997—Accessed at http://www.dtic.mil/whs/directives/corres/html/302515 htm. For an extensive, current discussion of the MACA, see http://carlisle-www.army.mil/usawc/dclm/linkedtextchapters/CHAPTER23.pdf.

the Army relies on Installation Support Packages (ISP) at each installation and at Regional Medical Centers. An ISP contains a 30-day supply of doxycycline and ciprofloxacin. The Army has enough for 25 percent of the total catchment population (meaning 25 percent of active duty soldiers, their family members, and Army civilian employees) for that installation. A 15-day supply is kept at the installation, and the other 15-day supply is kept in reserve at the Regional Medical Center.[29]

It is possible that the use of the SNS by the DOD will create some real challenges for military. For instance, the DOD will use different criteria for starting forces on antibiotics if military personnel have to enter a contaminated environment or if they might be exposed to a contagious biological agent. The DOD comprises a younger, healthier population that is required to work long hours with no time-off, and, of course, the DOD doesn't have the same liability concerns that exist in the civilian population. Given their preeminent expertise in response to such threats as WMD, and the likelihood that they will be required to be in close proximity to the incident focus, the DOD may choose to put young, healthy soldiers on antibiotics when they are at very low risk, while civilians at much higher risk are not being treated, thus ensuring military personnel availability during all phases of incident response.

---

[29] The Office of the Surgeon General has centrally programmed and funded the Army's biodefense materiel since 1994. The US Army Medical Materiel Agency (USAMMA) has procured, stored, and maintained this materiel for the Army in strategic locations. The Marine Corps has consolidated its materiel into five centralized locations, while the Air Force and Navy maintain their CB materiel in decentralized unit locations. For details see http://www.acq.osd mil/cp/vol1-2003cbdpannualreport.pdf. Accessed February 2004.

# Emerging Issues

The SNS continues to occupy a critical position in the response plans of local, state, and Federal authorities for dealing with major crises involving medical intervention. The plans, policies, and procedures for its use have continued to be modified since its inception in 1999 and remain the subject of new proposals on an ongoing basis. Recent issues include:

**USPS Delivery.** On February 18, 2004, the U.S. Postal Service (USPS) announced developing plans to deliver antibiotics from the stockpile directly to residential addresses in the event of a catastrophic incident.[30] With assurances that the procedures under consideration would only augment existing state and local plans, HHS has touted the vast USPS infrastructure as a primary catalyst for the "doorstep delivery" campaign.

While home delivery would likely reduce the crunch on the public health system and even stem the "worried well" of panicked civilians, the resulting legal issues would be immense. Proper labeling and safety guidelines would need to be prepared in advance. Pervasive public education would become even more critical, and postal workers may need incentives to volunteer. Moreover, releasing large quantities of unsupervised antibiotics could have devastating effects on drug potency, and a stringent decision-making process must be in place to prevent delivery in circumstances short of national disaster.

**Project Bioshield.** In his 2003 State of the Union Address, the President announced Project Bioshield.[31] This initiative may significantly impact the future content of the stockpile and its use to support the medical response to an incident in the United States. The primary focus of Project Bioshield is to develop and make available modern, effective drugs and vaccines to protect against attack by chemical and biological weapons or other dangerous pathogens. The initiatives announced to date include: strengthening National Institutes of Health (NIH) development capabilities by speeding research and development on medical countermeasures; ensuring that resources are available to pay

---

[30] United States Postal Service - News Release No. 04-015—Available at www.usps.com/communications/news/press/welcome.htm. Accessed February 2004.

[31] White House Press Release of February 3rd 2003 — Available at www.whitehouse.gov/news/releases/2003/02/20030203.html. Accessed February 2004.

for next-generation medical countermeasures; and giving the FDA the ability to make promising treatments quickly available in emergency situations.

The first two initiatives are designed to provide new medical components that may be used in the stockpile, but these will not be available for some considerable time. Of more immediate potential value for the stockpile is the possibility that the FDA can enable existing drugs to be used in emergency situations for medical conditions beyond their current labeling and license. The agency can also use an expedited process to enable promising drugs to be available for use in a crisis, providing they meet the criteria for safety and presumed efficacy. The United States Senate's unanimous approval of Project Bioshield on May 19, 2004 was a critical step toward enlisting the biotechnology community in the fight against biological and chemical weapon attacks. Together with ongoing discussions in which the author and the director of the Center for Technology and National Security Policy have engaged Congress, Project Bioshield will be an integral component of how the SNS is modified in coming months. The next step will be to ensure better liability protections for companies that choose to develop biomedical countermeasures without FDA approval. Senators Joseph Lieberman, D-Conn., and Orrin Hatch, R-Utah, have already begun work on a bill (Bioshield II) to address this concern.[32]

**Private-Public Partnerships.** The 21-year-old group Business Executives for National Security, or BENS, seeks to address the difficulties of local SNS distribution. Through its "Business Force" initiative, BENS is working with New Jersey county governments to initiate a proof-of-concept exercise that would show how businesses could play a vital role in distributing vaccines and other needed medical supplies during a terrorist attack. Two member companies in cooperation with two New Jersey county governments will create a plan, work through roadblocks (such as liability), and test the plan with an exercise that engages business as well as the state and local government. BENS has identified many counties that do not have adequate plans in place for distribution and dispensing, or lack the facilities and staff to do so. Using businesses as "points of dispensing" could remedy this deficiency and save lives. The success of the project may indicate one direction that state and local authorities can take to address the logistical burden of distributing the stockpile during a future incident.

---

[32] "Project Bioshield," Editorial, Washington Post, May 24, 2004.

# Recommendations

Today there exists a pressing need for preparation on the part of state and local governments and health officials. The non-profit organization Trust for America's Health released a report stating that as of December 2003 only two states had sufficient workers to distribute Strategic National Stockpile supplies.[33] While some progress has been made since then, there are still remaining states with shortfalls. Without comprehensive plans for the receipt and distribution of a push package, or a properly educated staff that can manage the supplies, the SNS will not reach the public in a timely manner.

A summary of state SNS exercises to date can be acquired through the Association of State and Territorial Health Officials (ASTHO). The document, *Exercising the Strategic National Stockpile: Lessons Learned and Tools for Application*, features the experiences of eight states that have exercised their SNS plans, discusses common obstacles, and capably highlights the lessons learned from this first round of training.[34] In collaboration with ASTHO and the Strategic National Stockpile Program, the National Association for County and City Health Officials (NACCHO) has begun work on an interactive CD-ROM resource for local health departments that will provide information on SNS planning and preparations. NACCHO also has published *The National Pharmaceutical Stockpile: A Reference for Local Planners*, a helpful companion document to the CDC's *Guide for Planners*.[35] It is recommended that local authorities meet this obligation head on so as to prevent the failure of the SNS program in the last step of planning.

The SNS is a critical component of the Nation's response to any future medical emergency, and it will be the subject of revision and refinement as our responses to such incidents advance. The key role of the SNS will endure, however, and the fact that it can be deployed at anytime and to anywhere in the continental United States is a tribute to those who conceived and built the stockpile to safeguard the country and its citizens.

---

[33] Ready or Not?: Protecting the Public's Health in the Age of Bioterrorism, (Washington, DC: TFAH, December 2003)—Available at http://healthyamericans.org/state/bioterror/Bioterror.pdf. Accessed March 2004.

[34] Exercising the Strategic National Stockpile: Lessons Learned and Tools for Application (Washington, DC: ASTHO, January 2004)—Available at http://www.astho.org/pubs/Exercisingthestockpile.pdf. Accessed March 2004.

[35] " The National Pharmaceutical Stockpile (NPS): A Reference for Local Planners" (Washington, DC: NACCHO)—Available at http://www.naccho.org/files/documents/NACCHO-NPS-Guide.pdf. Accessed January 2004.